Is the Moon the Center of the Universe?

By the same author:

HISTORY OF RUSSIA & THE SOVIET UNION in Humorous Verse
MAKE MARZIPAN, NOT WAR: Crazy Rhymes for Crazy Times
CHEESE PIRATES: Humorous Rhymes for Adult Children
CAFÉ BOMBSHELL: The International Brain Surgery Conspiracy
PETS OF THE GREAT DICTATORS & Other Works

Is the Moon the Center of the Universe?

A Reassessment of Many Things in Humorous Verse

Sabrina P. Ramet

Washington, DC

Copyright © 2016 by Sabrina P. Ramet

New Academia Publishing, 2017

All rights reserved. No part of this book may be reproduced or transmitted in any form or by any means, electronic or mechanical, including photocopying, recording, or by any information storage and retrieval system.

Printed in the United States of America

Library of Congress Control Number: 2017931618
ISBN 978-0-9981477-9-6 paperback (alk. paper)

 An imprint of new Academia Publishing
4401-A Connecticut Ave. NW, #236, Washington DC 20008

 info@newacademia.com
www.newacademia.com

In honor of Galileo Galilei (1564-1642)

Contents

ASTRONOMY & OTHER SCIENCE ... 1
Golf balls in orbit ... 3
Is the moon the center of the universe? ... 4
The secret of long life ... 5
The secret history of Duncan MacDougall ... 7
Gastrophysics ... 8
Welcome, extraterrestrials! ... 9
The future of theater in black holes ... 10
The universe is expanding ... 11
"Show me a sane man, and I will cure him for you" ... 12
Oh where, oh where has the universe gone? ... 13
Fluorescent toothpaste ... 15

RELIGION ... 17
In the confessional ... 19
Why are there no fallen fairies? ... 22
Let me out of here ... 23
Birthday beads ... 24
Pink's the sacred color ... 25
O mamma, are you a virgin? ... 26
Cafeteria Catholic ... 27
Plenary indulgence ... 28
My 13 male friends plus Luke ... 29
Saint Todd, patron saint of looking cool ... 30
Wasserspiel ... 31
Church-run brothels ... 32

THE ADVENTURES OF MICK AND BUTCH	33
The Adventures of Mick and Butch, Part One	35
Sayings, or the Adventures of Mick and Butch, Part Two	36
The Adventures of Mick and Butch, Part Three, or Absence makes the heart grow fonder	37
The Adventures of Mick and Butch, Part Four	39
THERE'S MOLD IN YOUR HAIR	41
Moldilocks and the three stares	43
Alice in mold land	44
Deck the halls with boughs of fungus	45
The universe is full of mold	46
"CHRISTMAS" SONGS	47
O Tannlege	49
Dental work in Tijuana	51
Christmas in Hawaii	52
That sinking feeling once again	53
Pancho Villa	54
Father Christmas and Mr. Holly	56
Santa is smart	58
TRAVEL & ART	59
Hotel Gabrovo	61
Gonna ride the big one soon	63
Haircuts in Honolulu	64
Is there a duck on board?	66
Mona Mia	68
I'm gonna sail to Liechtenstein	70
Welcome to the University of Bangkok	72
Aldwych Station	73

AT HOME, AT WORK, AND DINING OUT	75
Should I be concerned?	77
I want my son to join the army	78
Gourmette cuisine (oh, you wanted *gourmet* cuisine!)	79
My refrigerator gives me the cold shoulder	81
My father told me	82
I know what you're thinking	83
Cute as a button	84
Yeah, happy brush!	85
The meeting	86
Shampoo causes insanity	87
HISTORY	89
The Mayan calendar	91
Mad Anthony Wayne	93
The Battle of Marston Moor	95
Joanna the Nutty	96
Onward, Leif!	97
The last of the Habsburgs	98
The 'real' False Dimitry	99
Bowling Tudor style	100
CHILDREN'S RHYMES	101
On Dumpledy-Down	103
Alice in Limerickland	104
Knightsalot of the Round Table	109
Bedouin	110
Danger! Beware of the coconuts!	111
ANIMALS	113
Some of my best friends	115
My neighbor worships my dog	117

Caring for your jellyfish	118
My little 'font' goldfish	119
POLITICS AND MEDIA	121
Don't you be sexing, here in Uganda	123
Radio Walla Walla, best news team in the business	124
Chick chicky boom	125
Baa-baa, mad king	126
In praise of Erna	127
Choir wars with flutes	128
Silvio Berlusconi's paradise	129
A guide on how to riot	130
SUPERHEROES	131
The Adventures of Retread Rabbit	133
Rabbit Hood	134
The Lone Rabbit	135
Mighty Rabbit's on the way	136
Radioactive me	137
RAMBLINGS	139
About Petter Jenssen	141
Yo-ho yo, a professor's life for me	142
I just can't help myself	143
anARchisTs 4 gOOd grammar	144
Just so	145
For persons struggling with French words	146
You are not an individual	147
And	148
Jack and Jim went up the hill – no, that's not right	149
Stealing Being and Time	150
Procrastinator	151

The Great Stink of 1858	152
Bonk Bonk Bonk	153
Petrol station greeter	154

ASTRONOMY AND OTHER SCIENCE

Golf balls in orbit

(Composed on 6 December 2013, on Lufthansa flight LH 158, while parked on the runway at Frankfurt Airport, waiting for the signal to fly to Leipzig.)

Jupiter is far away with 67 moons,
I want to buy a ticket so I may visit soon.
One of them is Titon, where golfing is the craze;
they're playing golf for ages there, it's more than just a phase.
But gravity is low out there: when golfers hit their balls,
they fly out into orbit – no boundaries, no walls.
I have a telescope at home, have looked in that direction,
I've counted seven hundred balls in Jupiter's connection.
Somehow – I've determined – some of them have moss,
that means there must be water and here I'll add a gloss:
I'm looking for intelligence on golf balls out in space,
I know it would be rather small and with a tiny face.
But just imagine what we'd learn about what we could do
with golf balls still on planet earth, soaking in the dew.
So next time you go golfing, don't think of homegrown strife;
but check your golf ball closely: it might have signs of life.

Is the moon the center of the universe?

(Composed on 28 June 2014, between 22:30 and 22:53, while watching a documentary on the Discovery Channel about the prospects for human colonization of Mars.)

We know for sure the sun does not
rotate around the earth,
among so many reasons just
assess the solar girth.
But do some complicated math,
you might revise your thinking
and reach some new conclusions
before your eyes stop blinking:
the sun revolves around the moon,
just like the earth and Mars,
and likewise all the universe,
its asteroids and stars.
The only thing that puzzles me
is why there is resistance
to this so simple veritude,
but count on my persistence.

The secret of long life

(To be sung to the melody of "16 tons", a song popularized by Tennessee Ernie Ford, but also performed by Johnny Cash, Willie Nelson, and Tom Jones, among others. Composed on 1 August 2014.)

Some people say a man oughta drink alcohol,
Wine every day makes you healthy and whole,
It relaxes your body and sharpens your mind,
And quality wine is easy to find.

Old Jake Pickens thought what he'd been told,
Was the Gospel truth til the day he grew old.
Wine bottles in the kitchen, and he was sure,
That he owed his life to wine as a cure.

Other people say that alcohol's bad,
Better to avoid it, lest it drive you mad,
It hurts your liver and dulls your brain,
Before you know it, you are half insane.

Old Suzie Mae agreed with all that,
Never drank spirits or wine from the vat,
When she reached the age of a hundred and two,
The reason, she thought, was her milk-shake brew.

Still other folk "know" you should get lotsa sleep,
Just like on your back and count the sheep.
The longer you doze, the longer you live,
This is th'advice that some folks give.

Ole Billy Bob spent his life in bed,
Scarcely got up til the day he was dead.
When he reached the age of a hundred and four,
The reason he thought was "sleep and snore".

Ya know it's gotta be that others disagree,
Too much sleep robs your energy.
It destroys your muscles and erases your mind,
You don't need to sleep just to unwind.

Old Debbie Daisy didn't like to snooze,
She skipped the colas and she skipped the booze.
She stayed awake til a hundred and one,
And by staying awake, she had more fun,
And by staying awake, she had more fun.

The Secret History of Duncan MacDougall

(Composed on 11—12 October 2013.)

Duncan MacDougall, a scientist of note,
in silk shirt and bow-tie and woven frock coat,
wanted to prove that people had souls
and feeling so lucky he was on a roll.

He went to St. Mary's, where people were dying,
he hoped they'd be ready to do some complying.
He wanted to put them on feather-weight scales
and measure what happened when their souls took sail.

He had to be ready, no use to be late,
if he wanted to measure their difference in weight
from when they were living to when they were dead,
while lying there motionless on St. Mary's bed.

What he discovered in nineteen-oh-one
was that their weight changed when they were done:
lighter they were, by the measures he had,
though to be sure it was just by a tad.

"Aha!" he exclaimed, "I have proven my theory
that people have souls." It was nothing too eerie.
But dogs, when they died, did not change in weight –
how could MacDougall *that* explicate?

Oh, easy again, since dogs don't have souls,
and nor do amphibians, reptiles or moles.
But cats, I would wager, most certainly do:
I'm telling you this because it is true.

Gastrophysics

(Composed on 26 February 2015.)

What goes down must come up,
put the universe in your cup,
just don't drink it, silly pup.
What goes down must come up.

In the night sky there's a comet,
if you eat too much, you'll vomit.
In the black hole something's missing –
after lunch it's time for kissing.

Physics is the science of motion,
in your stomach some commotion.
There's a quasar in my bed,
it's only vomiting I dread.

What goes down must come up,
put the universe in your cup,
just don't drink it, silly pup.
What goes down must come up.

Welcome, extraterrestrials!

(Composed in Kalas & Canasta café in Trondheim on 14 February 2015, while waiting for our lunch to be served, and reflecting on the announcement by SETI officials that they would like to beam information about our planet into outer space.)

Greetings from Planet Earth to anyone out in space,
come on down and meet us.
We think that we are really smart,
so come on down and eat us.
We want to know who lives in space,
we're curious about your alien face.
We've thought through all our options,
and, yes, we are taking a chance.
If you care to visit us,
please start your stay in France.
Here in the United States of A,
some folks are rather worried,
but if you care to visit us,
we're sure you won't be sorry.
And as for us, shucks, we're not sure:
for our curiosity, you're the cure.
So, welcome extraterrestrials,
come on down and visit.
Land your spaceship anywhere –
here's the runway, you can't miss it.

The future of theater in black holes

(Composed in the evening on 30 December 2014.)

We've all read about the holes,
dark and black and, as we're told,
nothing there at all to see:
travel there, get bored, grow old.
But look – there's innovative stuff
presented there on Friday nights.
Buy a ticket, get in line,
take your seat, turn out the lights.
Yes, the black holes have their fun,
got to climb inside and see,
but looking 'cross the evening sky
I'm not sure where I want to be.
Which black hole is best for *Hamlet?*
Which is best for Bernard Shaw?
Are the actors all accomplished –
do they act without a flaw?
Are their theaters brightly lit?
Are their theaters better there?
Can I come in casual dress?
Do they offer better fare?
Why do scientists stay so silent
'bout the theaters out in space?
Surely folks on other planets
gonna have a time and place
for some evening entertainment
in their black holes in the skies.
Scientists know this, I am sure,
'cause they're clever, smart, and wise.

The universe is expanding

(Composed on 31 December 2014.)

The universe is expanding – I read it in a book
or maybe it was on TV. Just wait, I'll have a look.
The stars are moving farther out, completely out of reach –
as many stars and galaxies as sand grains on the beach.
Our town's expanding also, distances are greater –
you used to get to work on time, but now you'll get there later.
The shopping mall was once so near, now it's far away –
I used to reach it in an hour, now it takes all day.
There's good news though, abundantly, and this is very clear:
my closest neighbor's house has moved and is no longer here.
Twenty billion people – there's room for them and more,
the whole earth is expanding and there's plenty room next door.

"Show me a sane man, and I will cure him for you" – Carl Gustav Jung

(composed on 14 September 2013)

Psychiatrists have lots of books,
they look at them when no one looks.
Freud and Adler, Horney too,
here they find what's right and true.
Jung, Carl Gustav – well, he tried
but, as you know, his brain was fried.
Mystical, he was, and more:
reading him, I always snore.
What they know, they know for sure,
they're always ready with a cure.
Neurosis, schizo, bit depressed?
Take some advice and have a rest.
Paranoia raging wild?
Just unleash your inner child!
At the end of every day,
they're content they've had their say.

Oh where, oh where has the universe gone?

(In the course of a 28 May 2014 broadcast of "Through the Wormhole", host Morgan Freeman observed that most of the universe was "missing". More precisely, he cited scientific research arguing that what we can see and study amounts to just 4.6% of the universe. Another 0.4% consists of neutrinos – don't ask! – 23% of our old friend dark matter – said to contain metastable particles called "chameleons" – and the remaining 72% of dark energy. This computation suggested to those preparing Freeman's script that most of the universe was not available for study and thus, in a word, "missing". I wrote the following verse immediately after watching the show, setting it to the tune of "Oh where, oh where has my little dog gone", a rhyme written by composer Septimus Winner (1827–1902) together with its well-known tune. This verse is dedicated to Winner.)

Oh where, oh where, has the universe gone?
Oh where, oh where, can it be?
I'm floating along on a dark matter bed,
with chameleons deep in my head.

I think that we live
in a formula,
'cause mass is really (just) math,
and reality may well not be real:
just think about that in your bath.

Oh where, oh where has the universe gone?
5%'s not enough –
it's dark energy that accounts for most
of all of the universe stuff.

I think I will go to Lost and Found,
maybe I'll have luck there.
Maybe some citizen turned it in,
but if it's not there, then where?

Oh where, oh where has the universe gone?
If it's missing, is it my fault?
If it's found, I'll be so very relieved,
I'll start to turn somersaults…

Oh where, oh where has the universe gone?
If it's missing, is it my fault?

Fluorescent toothpaste

(Composed on 20 March 2015; modest revisions on 28 March 2015. After I had written about half of this verse, I was surprised to find that it could be sung to the tune of "Puttin' on the Ritz", a song written by Irving Berlin in 1929.)

Would you like your teeth to glow,
would you like your teeth to show
even in the darkest night,
giving off fluorescent light?
Bright teeth and never dentures,
no plaque and did we mention
that this toothpaste might
emit most unnatural light?
If your tooth is coming loose
and you don't want to cook the goose,
what you don't want
is pulling out the tooth.

Different teeth are in your mouth,
and you don't want to take them out –
our dentists like
pulling out the tooth!
Yes, they are fluorescent top to bottom
wearing luminescent gowns of cotton –
"rubber ducky" –
come let's brush
with new fluorescent paste
and you will see
that you'll avoid the awful fate of
pulling out the tooth!
pulling out the tooth!
pulling out the tooth!

RELIGION

In the confessional

(Composed on 19-20 February 2015. For Chris.)

Sinner: Bless me, father, for I have sinned,
more transgressions in the wind.
Two weeks now are in the bin,
since my last confession: here are my sins.
I was having a lark, just lying around,
so I fed the lark and went into town.
I needed some cash, so I went to the bank,
for the queue so long, whom should I thank?
But I wasn't prepared to wait too long,
and so I raised my voice, shouting "Honga pong-pong!"
I brandished my lark and a fish that stank,
and with that succeeded in robbing the bank.
As I finished, I spied a cop by the door,
so I kicked him in the shins and he dropped to the floor.
Bless me, father, that is all I can remember.

Priest: Well, my son, surely you have tweaked
the truth a little, since in just two weeks,
it is hard to believe you'd slip into sin,
robbing a bank – what made you begin?
And just two weeks, are you quite sure
that you were just here for a salvific cure?

Sinner: Yes, reverend father, I am quite certain,
I remember your confessional and your dark cotton curtain.
But I'm a nice fellow, not nasty or mean,
so give me absolution and wipe my slate clean.

Priest: Well, OK, but your tale is very scary –
for your absolution you should say a "Hail Mary".

Two hours later
Sinner: Bless me father, I'm a winner,
but every now and then, a sinner.
I did the penance you exacted
but soon after got distracted.
It has been two hours since my last confession, here with you,
and these are my sins.

Priest: Well, almighty God is gracious
and his heart is truly spacious.
But I'm not God and I can't see
why you're sinning so merrily.
Just two hours and now you're back!
You're probably a kleptomaniac!

Sinner: Not this time, most reverend father,
and believe me please that I would rather
sun myself on sandy beaches
or scratch my skin to pull out leaches,
than have to ask for absolution
yet again and in rhymed locution.
But as I left your celestial building,
I spied your altar with its golden gilding.
So I rolled it down the aisle, cluck-cluck,
and loaded it onto my pick-up truck.
Then I headed to the police station
in a state of most extreme elation.
I've always liked the front desk there
and the police chief's swivel chair.
So I rolled them out the station's door:
the police don't have them any more.
These were heavy but, cluck-cluck,
I loaded them onto my pick-up truck.
I'll sell this furniture some day
and post these items on ebay.

Bless me, though I may have omitted
other sins which I committed
in the two hours I've been gone –
so absolve me please and let's move on.

Priest: Well, stealing from the Church, your mother,
rather than from some other –
this is serious and it's quite perverse
and, yes, it's even somewhat worse
than robbing banks and kicking shins:
these are, in fact, substantial sins.
But three "Hail Marys" might suffice,
provided you promise to be nice
and your sinning to decrease.
You are forgiven: go in peace.
…
By the way, let me know when you post my altar on ebay.

Why are there no fallen fairies?

(Composed on 18 November 2014, late morning.)

Why are there no fallen fairies? –
they always do just what they should.
We all hear of fallen angels,
who've given up on being good.

But ask yourself where fairies live –
why all of them on lily pads!
This must be why they stay so happy,
and why they're never ever bad.

For lily pads have magic power,
which the fairies draw upon,
while fallen angels live in hellfire –
no magic there that can be won.

Frogs as well, on lily pads,
figure that they've got it all!
And now you know the reason why
no fairies ever took a fall.

Let me out of here

(Composed on 16 August 2014.)

God comes to see me each Wednesday at ten –
it's 9:55 and He's coming again,
sometimes with angels, sometimes alone,
but always with fireworks surrounding his throne.
I've always liked fireworks, they light up the sky,
though they make me feel hungry and I don't know why,
but just when I start to crave cheese-bread and tea,
God grows a bit bigger, starts talking to me.
He tells me astronomers have it all wrong:
the universe hasn't been 'round very long,
there wasn't a big bang, it happened instead
when God fashioned the cosmos from ideas in his head.
Evolution? Forget it! Why should God wait,
when He's got the power to put on his plate
exactly the things that He'd like to see –
the earth and the coconuts, oceans and sea.
He told me, as well, 'bout the rules we should follow,
if you don't believe me, your head must be hollow.
Virginity's good – but only for women –
with chasteness and modesty they should be brimmin'.
Go to the church and sit in the pews:
man, that's so obvious, it shouldn't make news.
This straightjacket's tight! Why must I wear it?
Take it off now – I just can't bear it.
Listen to me, 'cause I know it all,
let me out of here quickly and don't you dare stall.

Birthday beads

(Composed 16 April 2014.)

For my birthday I got a rosary,
matches the color of my hosiery.
Sundays I'm in church in Leeds,
where I swing my rosary beads.
Every morning I say a prayer,
I want to be a demon-slayer.
I hate evil, I like good,
my favorite saint is Robin Hood.
I'm not sure 'bout the parish priest,
he doesn't seem serious about the Beast.
Seems like Satan's everywhere,
at least there's incense in the air.
I like to go to Sunday Mass,
especially when there're choir and brass.
I make sure I'm nicely dressed –
Boy, I'm thrilled when I get blessed.

Pink's the sacred color

(Composed between 30 September and 4 October 2014. Inspired by a tiny cult in Japan which requires that its members dress in white and drive around in white vans.)

I'm founding a religion (you will not have to think),
just take me as your leader and dress yourself in pink.
Pink's the sacred color – a group of angels told me:
they said I should profess the faith, while always acting boldly.
I've written up a holy book in meter and in rhyme,
I'll read insightful passages and you can play the mime.
My van is pink and shiny, so we can drive around
and spread the words we have on hand.
Let's go: we're homeward bound!
We have a pair of sacraments:
for men, we probe the prostate,
and for women anal probes suffice –
sufficient cause to celebrate.
Our other sacrament is this,
a fixture of our creed –
we sit around on stools and listen
to the music of Dean Reed.
For us he is a living saint,
even though he's dead,
and every night we think of him
as we go to bed.

O mamma, are you a virgin?

(Composed on 18 July 2014, late evening. This may be sung as blues song.)

I get up mornings and ask myself,
Who's my father? – that great elf,
in the sky or some other,
who had sex with you, dear mother?
O mamma, are you a virgin?
Hey mamma, are you a virgin?

It happened once, I know for certain,
a virgin birth – up went the curtain!
And if a first time, why not twice?
What are the odds? – just roll the dice!
O mamma, I'm eatin' sturgeon,
O mamma, are you a virgin?

Is my father really Dad?
I have a theory that makes me glad:
it just could be I'm the Son of God –
don't look at me as if I'm odd!
O mamma, God is a surgeon,
Hey mamma, are you a virgin?

Cafeteria Catholic

(In the old days, Catholic priests would use the expression "cafeteria Catholic" to refer to a person who, although baptized a Catholic, nonetheless did not accept all the doctrines of the Church. Composed on 30 July 2014.)

He gets in line, with tray in hand,
knows there are things he cannot stand.
He grabs a dish of God as trinity,
but leaves the side-dish of Christ's divinity.
He somehow thinks that that makes sense,
but infallible popes just make him tense.
But Immaculate Conception on a plate
is like a salad of Mary's fate.
Twelve apostles – that's too few,
surely Christ needed thirty-two
or maybe more and who's to know?
But twelve is a figure much too low.
The crucifixion, that's okay –
as a soup, he means to say.
A glass of heaven, cup of hell –
what's that he's adding? He won't tell!
On his tray there's still some space,
so he loads up on lots of grace.
Comes the time to pay the check,
his lunch is small: so what the heck!

Plenary indulgence

(Composed on 12 December 2014. This verse no longer includes sexual language, as that has been censored. However, parental guidance is suggested, especially for persons over age 50.)

For a plenary indulgence, you'll feel the effulgence
of grace straight from heaven to you.
The collection plate's coming, give cash, not just humming
then stand, kneel, and sit in the pew.
For sins that are weighty, the price is now eighty –
that's dollars, not kroner today.
So shout "halleluyah", in old Walla Woolya,
the deacon is ready to pray.

My 13 male friends plus Luke

(Composed on 17 September 2014.)

My best friend is Matthew Mark,
playing pool he's quite a shark.
Another friend is also Jude,
like Andrew, he is never lewd.
Luke likes John and John likes James,
while Peter mixes up their names.
Bartholemew does not talk much,
at least not since that special touch
from Simon, who stays home a lot.
Then there is Iskariot –
he and Philip march about,
while Thomas likes to sit and doubt.
I asked him why he liked to doubt,
he answered thus, that Luke was "out".
"Replace him with another James" –
so two close friends – well, check their names.
These are the men whom I hold close,
but women, well, I like the most.

Saint Todd, patron saint of looking cool

(Composed in March 2015.)

If you want a better bod,
say a prayer to Saint Todd,
patron saint of looking cool.
Soon, you'll see the ladies drool,
when they see your eyebrows flicker –
that's the headline and the kicker.
Would you like to reduce fat?
Dear Saint Todd can help with that.
Would you like a firmer chin?
Contact Todd, perhaps he's in.

Wasserspiel

(In the glorious baroque period, the Archbishop of Salzburg had a palace built for himself known as Hellbrunn Palace. The archbishop was a jokester, and had a concrete table and chairs set up in his garden, so that he might entertain himself at his guests' expense, with his Wasserspiel or Water Game. This verse celebrates the archbishop's sense of humor. Composed on 30 March 2015.)

The bishop had some guests come 'round to join him and his daughter,
he thought it would be lots of fun to drench them all in water.
They sat around the table and when the food was coming,
the bishop turned a little crank connected to the plumbing.
Their chairs had little holes through which the water came out gushing,
and as their butts got soaking wet, the bishop started blushing.
"What do you think," the bishop asked, "and, yes, what do you feel?
'Cause this is what I like to call my little Wasserspiel."

Church-run brothels

(In the 1300s and 1400s, Church-run brothels proliferated in Central Europe. A program on the History Channel attributed the initiative for this phenomenon to one Johann (John) of Salzburg, who believed that the brothels could encourage men to prefer sex with women over sex with other men, while, at the same time, helping to promote Christianity. The following verse, composed on 20 April 2015, offers some reflections on this theme. The verse is set to the music of "Happy days are here again", a song composed in 1929, with music by Milton Ager and lyrics by Jack Yellen.)

Church-run brothels in your town –
they banish sadness and your frown,
and the prostitutes discuss the faith:
happy brothels in your town.

John of Salzburg – he was smart –
he learned Church doctrines from a tart,
and he thought that was the way to start
a religious class for men.

He hoped as well that these whirls
would get men attracted to girls,
hey –

Church-run brothels are the rage,
and they provide a healthy stage
for long discussions of the faith –
happy brothels come of age!

THE ADVENTURES OF MICK & BUTCH

The Adventures of Mick and Butch, Part One

(Started on 21 February 2014.)

Blood is thicker than water.
Butch wanted to put this to a scientific test; so he stabbed Mick on the arm and took a sample.
A cat has nine lives.
Mick thought he would put this to the test, and threw Butch's cat out the window; apparently the saying is wrong.
An elephant never forgets.
Butch wanted revenge for his cat and tried to throw Mick's elephant out of its 8th story window. He did not succeed and the elephant never forgave Butch.
It's possible to have too much of a good thing,
Mick was not convinced of this, and gave Butch 50 cats for Christmas.
Good things may come when you least reject them:
That was Butch's motto, and he accepted the cats.

Sayings, or The Adventures of Mick and Butch, Part Two

(Composed on 24 December 2013.)

You can't make an omelette without breaking legs.
Mick wanted some breakfast, so he knee-capped Butch.
Every shroud has a silver lining –
which explains why Butch stole shrouds.
The Mass is always meaner on the other side –
which explains why Mick did not convert to Satanism.
You can lead a hearse to the water, but you cannot make it sink:
Butch had a different opinion, and sank the hearse, with Mick's body in it.
Where there's a will, there's an inheritance;
unfortunately for Butch, Mick had not left him anything.

The Adventures of Mick and Butch, Part Three, or Absence makes the heart grow fonder

(Composed on 5-6 September 2014.)

Butch was feeling very sick,
because he missed his best friend, Mick.
He was crying into his breakfast
and could not see the porridge for the bees.
Being is relieving – he realized now.
Burley and dead, burley surprise, makes a man stealthy but full of lies:
Mick had been burley, now he was dead,
and Butch had been lying to himself in bed.
Dead men tell no tales? He didn't believe it,
and went to a séance to try to achieve it,
to make contact with Mick, who told him only,
"Some people are better left undead."
Then – even worse – his girlfriend Gail
had been nabbed by police and hauled off to jail,
so he went to the jailer and asked, "What's up?"
The man replied, "A bitch in crime does time."
"What can I do to get her out?"
"Funny chalks," he heard the man shout.
So he went out shopping for blue, red, and green,
yellow, and purple chalk, with a glimmering sheen.
He returned to the jailer with a bag full of chalks,
thought to himself, "the more, the merrier."
But the jailer – he was not impressed:

"Everything comes to those who donate,"
the jailer started to translate.
So Butch paid the piper with cash, got her out,
to pay the jailer roundabout.

The Adventures of Mick and Butch, Part Four

(Composed on 14-15 February 2015. For anyone who may miss an allusion or two, clues as to the derivation of some of this apparent nonsense may be found immediately after this verse.)

Mick had confided many adventures, telling his dear friend Butch,
"If I should die, then write up my memoirs, so that the world may know,
That I was brave for a brainy day, and also that slime does not stay,
And though sleeping dogs don't lie to you, a silly filly may.
Tomato paste makes taste – it's true – in pizza and in life,"
but Mick did not live long enough to find himself a wife.
He'd flashed a smile, sailing down the Nile, composing couplets all the while.
Now he was gone, Butch missed him so, for Mick was ever so nice
and whenever the talk was slow to start, Mick knew how to bake the lice.
His life was, one may say, as knit as a riddle:
he was a bird watcher, with a pot in the farm.
But he also knew that a fixture is worth a thousand birds.
He took up skating
because everything comes to those who skate.
A friend and fellow skater was none other
than a cop in Nantucket.
And when, one day, a local parish asked Mick
to be their pastor,
he could not deny the appointment.

He was so smart
and could always separate the sheets from the coats.
He was an achiever, a clever perceiver,
and every then and now, a true upheaver.
But, Butch thought to himself, better fate than fever
and, in any event,
too many crooks oil the moth.

(Clues: save for a rainy day, crime does not pay, let sleeping dogs lie, haste makes waste, break the ice, fit as a fiddle, shot in the arm, a picture is worth a thousand words, everything comes to those who wait, drop in the bucket, fly in the ointment, separate the sheep from the goats, better late than never, too many cooks spoil the broth.)

THERE'S MOLD IN YOUR HAIR

Moldilocks and the Three Stares

(Inspired by reports of the reappearance of mold in Building 1 at Dragvoll, more than a decade since its first (?) appearance, and, rather obviously, by the children's story about one Goldilocks and the three bears. Composed in the evening on 5 March 2015.)

In a cottage in Lymington down by the shore
lived the Moldilocks girl – was she ever a bore!
There was mold on her table, her bed, and the floor,
there was mold in the oven, the closet, and door.
When guests came around by evening or night
sometimes they showed some symptoms of fright,
and alleged that the mold was an improper blight
but Moldilocks noted that mold too has rights.
One day as she sat by the window and gazed
out to the world to watch sheep as they grazed,
she suddenly sat up, surprised and amazed,
for the sheep looked quite looney and utterly crazed.
So she dished up some porridge to take to the sheep –
they lapped it up happily, then went to sleep
but not before staring, while burping beep-beep –
it all made her feel like Little Bo-Peep.
And when she looked 'round a mosquito was staring
straight at her face and surely was scaring
poor Moldilocks terribly, who soon was comparing
this feeling to recent nocturnal nightmaring.
Stares from the sheep and mosquitoes – what next?
It all made her feel so disbobbled and vexed
but you can be certain she felt quite perplexed
when a third stare was sent as an SMS text.
But porridge like borage appeals to some folk
especially to those whose thinking's baroque.
So "raise high the roofbeam" – this is no joke,
each has her yodel, each has her stroke.

Alice in mold land

(Composed around midnight, 26/27 February 2015.)

Alice was just 21,
didn't feel the least bit old,
when she discovered something fun:
a giant mountain made of mold.

A luminous path was circling 'round
this mountain to the very top.
She started walking, feet to ground,
so much mold, it felt like slop.

The mold got on her shoes and shirt
but she kept walking – it seemed clear
that if she only would exert,
she'd get to see the stratosphere.

She walked and walked and reached the crest,
and from the story I've been told,
it seems that looking east or west,
all she saw for miles was mold.

She remembered now and then she thought
that there was more to life than mold,
that this was not the goal she'd sought
and walked back down, or rather strolled.

Deck the halls with boughs of fungus

(Composed on 19 March 2015.)

Deck the halls with boughs of fungus
fa-la la-la-la, la-la la-la
breathe the spores into your lungus
fa-la la-la-la, la-la la-la.
Roll me now a fungus barrel
fa-la-la, fa-la-la, la la la
'tis the season to get moldy
fa-la la-la-la, la-la la-la.

Now the walls are full of fungus
fa-la la-la-la, la-la la-la
but we'll clean it up to-mungus
fa-la la-la-la, la-la la-la
then we'll make a huge bonfire
fa-la-la, fa-la-la, la-la-la
burn the mold upon the pyre
fa-la la-la-la, la-la la-la.

The universe is full of mold

(Composed on 21 April 2015, with minor modifications on 23 and 24 April 2015.)

The universe is very old –
hence, no surprise it's full of mold.
So don't believe what you've been told:
80% is pure dark mold.

"CHRISTMAS" SONGS

O Tannlege

(Composed in December 2013, in Norwegian, with translation following; to the tune of "O Tannenbaum").

O Tannlege, O Tannlege, så deilig er bedøvelsen.
Jeg liker ikke smerten min, jeg liker metallboren din.
O Tannlege, O Tannlege, så deilig er bedøvelsen.

O Tannlege, O Tannlege, så vakkert er kontoret ditt.
Ja, bordet ditt er veldig rent og spyttekumet – veldig pent.
O Tannlege, O Tannlege, så vakkert er kontoret ditt.

Oh Dentist, Oh Dentist, your anaesthetic is so delicious.
I don't like my pain, I like your metal drill.
Oh Dentist, Oh Dentist, your anaesthetic is so delicious.

Oh Dentist, Oh Dentist, your office is so beautiful.
Your table, yes, is very clean and your spit basin – very pretty.
Oh Dentist, Oh Dentist, your office is so beautiful.

Dental work in Tijuana (another Christmas song, of sorts)

(This verse should be sung to the tune of "White Christmas", melody by Irving Berlin. Composed on 28 June 2014; dedicated to JR, who loves Christmas songs.)

I've never been to Tijuana –
no, never ever in my life.
Well, OK, maybe, when I had rabies,
I may have been there once or twice.

I'm dreaming of a low-cost dentist,
with every cavity I get.
May your teeth be merry and white,
and may all your dental work delight.

You'll find the dentists there work cheaply,
at least the ones that don't pay tax.
If your teeth need fixing, the drinks are mixing,
just take a swig and then relax.

I've booked my flight to Tijuana,
I will be seated in the aisle.
In th'event we crash on our route,
my clean teeth will give me cause to smile.

Christmas in Hawaii

(To be sung to the tune of "Easter Parade" (1933), music & the original lyrics by Irving Berlin) (composed in summer 2013.)

It's Christmas in Hawaii – that's something you should try-ee,
sweet papayas's ready with some Oahu beers,
pineapple and guava – don't worry 'bout the lava,
the mountain's not erupted in some eighty odd years.

Honolulu turf, let's go out and surf,
The Great Frigatebirds will see us
and you'll be the rave on a gigantic wave.

I could dance a tango, to each and every quango,
that's come to old Hawaii on the government's tab.

Honolulu turf, let's go out and surf,
The Great Frigatebirds will see us
and you'll be the rave on a gigantic wave.

Oh, I could write a ballad about a Russian salad,
and not forget to tell you that I think that you're fab!

That sinking feeling once again

(Composed on 1 December 2014. Should be sung to the tune of "God Rest Ye Merry Gentlemen", a song originally written in the 15th century, with the earliest known publication occurring in 1760.)

I hope our nuclear submarine
has neither cracks nor leaks,
'cause if our sub had cracks or leaks,
then we'd be up the creek.
But creeks are four feet deep at most,
so we could climb right out.
Oh, tidings of gladness and joy, gladness and joy,
Oh, tidings of gladness and joy!

The sub commander told me that
he'd read some Thomas Hobbes.
He'd hoped that somehow that would help
to figure out the knobs
on all the panels in his sub –
he felt a bit confused.
Oh, tidings of madness ahoy, madness ahoy,
Oh, tidings of madness ahoy!

We made it to the bottom
but we wanted to go up.
The sub commander had no training –
he was just a pup.
He'd bought his license on the net
and specified his rank.
Oh, tidings of sadness but coy, sadness but coy,
Oh, tidings of sadness but coy!

Pancho Villa

(Set to the tune of «Angels, we have heard on high»; started on 1 December, completed on 9 December 2014.)

Pancho Villa, we have heard
that your exploits have incurred
Huerta's anger – that is true –
after he had staged a coup.
Your heroism, your heroism, your heroism is so great,
we are all inspired.
Your heroism, your heroism, your heroism is so great,
we are all inspired.

Speaking very candidly,
you started out with banditry.
Fighting for the working class,
you never let injustice pass.
Yes champion of the, yes champion of the, yes champion of the working class,
Yes, you helped the working class.
Yes champion of the, yes champion of the, yes champion of the working class,
Yes, you helped the working class.

Talent scouts, well, they came forth
to film your battles in the north,
you will see your name in lights,
and films about your glorious fights.
Yes, Hollywood has, yes Hollywood has, yes Hollywood has interest,
in your great adventures.
Yes, Hollywood has, yes Hollywood has, yes Hollywood has interest,
in your great adventures.

E. Zapata was your friend,
You both pursued a common end.
You 'scaped from prison once or twice,
and fought against evil and vice.
Down with diabolic, down with diabolic, down with diabolic politics!
Long live niceness everywhere!
Down with diabolic, down with diabolic, down with diabolic politics!
Long live niceness everywhere!

Father Christmas and Mr. Holly

(When I was living in London as a youngster, my mother would take me just before Christmas to Selfridges on Oxford Street, a prominent department store in downtown London, to visit with Father Christmas, who would hold court in that establishment during Yuletide. There was always a little adventure involved, such as a ride on a "submarine", where the children would sit in rows, while bubbles would be blown on the other side of fake portholes. Then, before we could meet with Father Christmas, we had a chance to talk with his friend, Mr. Holly, a fine gentleman who was always attired entirely in green. This verse, composed in tribute to those delightful experiences of my childhood, may be sung to the tune of "God rest ye merry gentlemen". Composed early morning on 12 January 2016)

Old Father Christmas has a friend, I've seen him in the shop.
His name is Mr. Holly and he used to be a cop,
but now he dresses all in green and dances til he drops,
oh tidings of gladness and zen, gladness and zen,
oh yes, these two are very happy men.

In Selfridges, the mezzanine, these two men have their stead,
Mr. Holly cooks their meals, while St. Nick makes the bed,
and every Friday afternoon the two men bake some bread.
oh tidings of flour and of yeast, flour and yeast,
yes, it's time to plan another Christmas feast!

But then one day Americans claimed that they had found
Father Christmas' long-lost wife, wandering around.
Mrs. Claus, she called herself, but who was Mr. Claus?
oh Mr. Holly got concerned and even rather depressed,
oh tidings of worries from the West.

But Father Christmas reassured his life-long friend and said,
he didn't know this "Mrs. Claus" and never'd shared his bed
with her or any of her friends and rather would be dead,
than to lose what the two-oo men had shared, two men had shared,
and old Mr. Holly shouldn't have despaired.

This "Mrs. Claus" has gone away and lives in Redwood Falls,
she's found a Minnesotan man, a handsome man and tall.
On weekends they just walk around the city's shopping malls.
oh tidings of shopping at the malls, shopping at malls,
then at bowling alleys, rolling down some balls.

Old Father Christmas has a friend, I've seen him in the shop.
His name is Mr. Holly and he used to be a cop,
but now he dresses all in green and dances til he drops,
oh tidings of gladness and zen, gladness and zen,
oh yes, these two are very happy men.

Santa is smart

(Composed in early January 2016.)

Santa is smart and he knows that
you can't play cricket with a baseball bat.
And if you think ice hockey's nice,
don't try dancing when you're on the ice.
Santa knows all sorts of stuff
especially sports played kinda rough.
Santa's taught his reindeer how
to play at polo when they're on a cow.

TRAVEL & ART

Hotel Gabrovo (International Joke Capital of the World, and of Europe)

(Composed on 25 August 2014; minor modifications on 26 and 27 August. For Thomas Berker.)

Welcome here in our hotel,
where our pleasures can be your pleasures.
We are proud to announce, darling guests,
that our hotel has not been attacked by terrorists
since 2008.
Rooms all equipped with beds and lamps.
Desks and chairs available on request.
Toilet down the hall, as well as bath.
Telephone service Mondays through Fridays:
weekends are off for telephone operator --
as she deserves, you will agree, guest darling.
No television in room,
but live entertainment in your room upon request.
We regret that dead entertainer was in room 23
some years back,
but he has since been fired and corpse removed,
along with day manager.
OK, it happened once -- but nothing happened,
since he was already dead.
Check out the indoor/outdoor training center
on fifth floor, complete with simulated bus.
Swimming pool very convenient --
an easy 20-minute bus ride
on mostly paved road.
Snakes along road? no worry:
we shoot them for you.

Elevators have been reinforced and electrified
for your safety.
Staircase upgraded, also new manager.
Throw towels on floor, we clean up --
or think of not wasting our water.
When leaving, give positive feedback:
last year, feedback was negative,
and entire staff was dismissed.
Good for us -- we have new jobs!
Welcome in our hotel!

Gonna ride the big one soon

(To be sung to the tune of "Dream a little dream of me" (1931), music by Fabian André & Wilbur Schwandt; the original lyrics were written by Gus Kahn. Composed in 2013.)

Sun beaming down above you,
it beckons me to Waikiki beaches,
birds singing in a pineapple mist –
gonna ride the big one soon.

I'm waxing down my surfboard,
I'm puttin' on my sun screen as well now,
I'm lookin' for a very good wave –
gonna ride the big one soon.

Sun's setting but I linger on, dear,
still craving the wave.
I'm ready to linger 'til dawn, dear,
just saying this:

I'm waxing down my surfboard,
I'm puttin' on my sun screen as well now,
I'm lookin' for a very good wave –
gonna ride the big one soon.

Haircuts in Honolulu

(Completed on 18 December 2013.)

I often travel to Hawaii, but never while awake,
I sleep, I dream, I dream some more, and then I take a break:
I'm flying to Hawaii on my Big Dog motorbike,
Coco Palms is where I land, and then I grab the mike.
I'm singing now, the crowd goes wild, they stomp their feet and cheer,
the owners are so happy, 'cause the people want more beer.
I've come to see the wildlife, the Hoary Bat no less,
but I end up in a barber shop, with my hair in quite a mess.
The barber stands there, smiles at me but always looking formal,
Says to me, "Just take a seat. Hello! I'm very normal.
Here's a coffee, sugar too, for gustatory sipping,
wait your turn, it's coming soon, and then we'll start some clipping."
I have this dream so often and I always hope to see,
some exotic flowers, wildlife, and beaches by the sea.
But every time I dream this dream, I see a distant harbor,
but head downtown and find myself once more with the barber.
This dream seems surrealistic and even paranormal,
But the barber simply greets me: "Hello! I'm very normal.
Here's a coffee, sugar too, for gustatory sipping,
wait your turn, it's coming soon, and then we'll start some snipping."
I try to tell the barber that he cut my hair last week,
but he nods so very sweetly and does not want to speak.
I try to find a therapist, but only in my dreams,
I don't need one in actual life, it's only what it seems.
But try to poke 'round Honolulu in a dreaming state,
You find an office, verify the name that's on the plate.
Therapy, the nameplate claims, but once you are inside,
You're looking at a barber, who's looking satisfied.
The barber stands there, smiles at me but always looking formal,

and then he simply greets me: "Hello! I'm very normal.
Here's a coffee, sugar too, for gustatory sipping,
wait your turn, it's coming soon, and then we'll start some clipping."

Is there a duck on board?

(Composed on 28 October 2013.)

I had to take a flight to Rome,
but didn't want to fly alone.
So I paid an extra buck
so I could bring along my duck.
When we got above the clouds,
a passenger was groaning loud,
sounded like he had bad luck,
but I just stroked by rider duck.

Then I heard it loud and clear:
"Do we have a duck up here?
'cause we've got a man who's sick,
now we need a duck real quick!"
How's my ducky going to help?
But I heard my neighbor yelp,
"There's a duck across the aisle,
and she has a charming smile."

Does my duck have special knowledge?
Did she graduate from college?
Is she licensed to assist?
Why does the stewardess persist?
But then I heard another fellow
stand up straight and start to bellow:
what he needed was a doc,
not a duck – that was a shock!

But the doctor was too late,
my duck'd refused to hesitate,
and brought the sick man back to health,
quacking secretly in stealth.
So next time you're not feeling well,
call my number, ring my bell:
if I find my duck is free,
I'll send her over, for a fee.

Mona Mia

(Composed in a few minutes after midnight on 1 March 2014, during a brief break from my slumber.)

Every Friday Jacques heads down
to see the paintings in his town.
See his stride, he's on the move,
again he's walking to the Louvre.

It's love, that's what it is – it's love!
And no, there is no shame,
if his beloved's in a frame.
It's love, that's what it is – it's love!

He sweeps into that magic room,
all is silence, like in a tomb.
He draws up close to see the painting:
Mona Lisa – now he's fainting.

Love, that's what it is – it's love!

Sweet Mona Lisa, she's his joy,
he just hopes that he's her boy.
She just sits there, with her smile
and no trace of grief or bile.

It's love, that's what it is – it's love!

He buys an easel, paint and brushes,
takes his time and then he rushes,
his self-portrait should find its place
to hang beside his sweetie's face.

It's love, that's what it is – it's love!

I'm gonna sail to Liechtenstein

(This verse is set to the meter of "Camptown Races", a song composed by Stephen Collins Foster (1826-1864). Composed on 18 November 2014, early morning.)

I'm gonna sail to Liechtenstein, doo-dah, doo-dah!
I know there's neither sea nor brine, oh doo-dah day!
Oh doo-dah day, oh doo-dah day,
I'm gonna sail to Liechtenstein, oh doo-dah day!

I'm settin' sail from Budapest, doo-dah, doo-dah!
I think I know the route that's best, oh doo-dah day!
Oh doo-dah day, oh doo-dah day!
I'm settin' sail from Budapest, oh doo-dah day!

So, load my ship on a flatbed truck, doo-dah, doo-dah!
I'm counting on my usual luck, oh doo-dah day!
Oh doo-dah day, oh doo-dah day!
So, load my ship on a flatbed truck, oh doo-.dah day!

I know the driver knows the way, doo-dah, doo-dah!
It's effortless to sail this way, oh doo-dah day!
Oh doo-dah day, oh doo-dah day!
It's effortless to sail this way, oh doo-dah day!

Welcome to the University of Bangkok

(Composed on 30 January 2014 at Trondheim-Værnes Airport while waiting for the 10:05 flight to Ålesund; revised during the flight. Dedicated to Stephen Fry, who does not believe that any city with the name Bangkok actually exists.)

This land is my land,
this land is Thailand.
We are all happy,
this is not cry-land.
No deadwood scholars
in this department:
Bangkok was made for you and me.

Aldwych Station

(Inspired by a short bit on the Travel Channel, highlighting an underground (tube) station in London, built in 1907 under the name "Strand Station" and later renamed "Aldwych Station." In order to construct the station, it was necessary to destroy the Strand Theatre, which was in fact the only reason anyone might have wanted to ride to that location. Plans to extend the track were abandoned and there were few passengers since there was not much to do besides wait for the next train to take one back whence one came. The station was closed in 1994.)

Aldwych Station – why was it built?
Enjoy your ride there, up to the hilt.
When you get there, nothing to do:
so leave the train and get in the queue.
Once a new train comes on track,
get on board and ride the train back
to where you started on this run –
now you've done it – wasn't that fun?

AT HOME, AT WORK, AND DINING OUT

Should I be concerned?

(Composed on 8 September 2014.)

My youngest child's first words were "Comrade Stalin" –
should I be concerned?
My dog has false teeth, but I have no idea how he got them –
should I be concerned?
My therapist has had a lobotomy –
should I be concerned?
All my neighbors had plastic surgery so that they could look just like me –
should I be concerned?
My spouse wants us to take our next vacation in the Bermuda triangle –
should I be concerned?

I want my son to join the army

(*Composed on 18 November 2014, early afternoon.*)

I want my son to join the army,
yes this matters – no mere trifle.
He should wear a uniform,
and lock and load his service rifle.
Though he's only three years old,
I've planned his future, and much more.
It's still too early to inform him
what the future holds in store.
But once he's ten or even eight,
I'll let him know what I have planned:
I know he will obey me always
and respect what I have banned.

Gourmette cuisine (oh, you wanted "gourmet" dining!)

(Composed on 14 November 2013, in the wee hours; for Morten Kulen.)

So you're wanting quesadilla –
that's a treat for you and me-ya.
Here's the way we make it here,
bet your mouth is watering, dear:
Fried tortilla, finger-lickin',
just add lettuce and some chicken,
half a teaspoon grated cheese,
sliced tomato if you please,
thousand island, what a treat!
Now it's ready, time to eat!

Chicken Kiev's so delicious,
and our recipe's ambitious.
We're proud our take is quite original,
using only foods indiginal.
Vodka floating on your plate,
lettuce that we'll rehydrate,
chicken and some grated cheese,
sliced tomato if you please,
thousand island, what a treat!
Now it's ready, time to eat!

Tacos? Yes, we serve that too:
big demand, get in the queue.
Our chief is such a cooking master,
was a time he was a pastor.
Some jalapenos start the brew,
bed of lettuce, chicken too,
sliced tomato if you please,

and a little grated cheese,
thousand island, what a treat!
Now it's ready, time to eat!

T-bone steak? Why that's our specialty,
and we make it nice and freshalty.
We're sure that you'll be quite awe-stricken
when you learn we're using chicken.
Sprinkle parsley all around,
lettuce, chicken – half a pound,
half a teaspoon grated cheese,
sliced tomato if you please,
thousand island, what a treat!
Now it's ready, time to eat!

My refrigerator gives me the cold shoulder

(Composed on 24 June 2014.)

My refrigerator is so cold,
though I confess – if truth be told –
I'm not so friendly with it either:
we don't have much we want to share.

But when I open the fridge's door,
sometimes I can hear it implore,
"Close it quickly, I'm getting hot.
Please don't let in so much air."

I've tried at times to start to chatter
about where to store the cheese and batter,
but my fridge has few opinions,
just likes to stand and quietly stare.

My father told me

(Composed within 5 minutes, a little after 7 p.m., on 2 August 2014, in a mountain cabin in Storli Valley, Norway.)

My father told me whales can speak,
but in fact just once a week.
My father told me lizards fly,
they sprout their wings, take to the sky.
My father told me pirates sing,
explicating everything.
My father told me I'll be queen,
my gown will have a silvery sheen.
My father told me that great deeds
are written down in books I read.
My father gave me seven pounds
and sent me out for coffee grounds.

I know what you're thinking

(Composed in my head while taking a foamy warm bath on a Sunday afternoon, 12 October 2014.)

I know what you're thinking,
and you know that I know what you're thinking.
Of course, I know that you know that I know what you're thinking,
and you know that I know that you know that I know what you're thinking.
Moreover, I know that you know that I know that you know that I know that you know that I know what you're thinking.
But do you know that you know what you're thinking?
Probably not.

Cute as a button

(Composed on 19 February 2014.)

Cute as a button – the saying is this.
But find me a button as cute as my miss.

Yeah, happy brush!

(Composed at high velocity the morning of 24 October 2014.)

A maiden on the misty heath
showing off her listy teeth,
An arc of triumph, crown of gold
fitted as an alginate mold.
Behold the mighty tube of paste,
with its apple-mango taste!
A brushing here, a brushing there
and there'll be no cavities anywhere!
Yeah, happy brush, none can withstand
your application by my hand.
Bacteria tremble, quake in fear
when my toothbrush draweth near.
Hail, toothbrush! I love your feel --
that's why I use you after every meal.

The meeting

(Being composed on 25 October 2014, to the tune of Julius Fucik's "The Entry of the Gladiators".)

Hey, we're gonna have an office meeting,
bring your pencils 'cause attention's fleeting.
If you don't write it,
you will forget it –
then you won't be able to contribute.

Hey, we're taking stock of office light bulbs,
in three hours we hope to just resolve this:
are they too bright now,
are they too dim?
Everyone's opinion counts!

Do you think that 60 watts is much too bright?
Do you think that 60 watts is much too dim?
Do you think we should use candles here?
'cause we want to hear your views –
Yes we do, yes we do, yes we do.

Do you think we should postpone this case?
Do you think we should discuss it more?
Should we think about alternatives?
'cause we want to hear all views –
Yes we do, yes we do!

Shampoo causes insanity

(Composed on 6 April 2015.)

Shampoo causes insanity – it soaks into your brain,
my neighbor uses shampoo daily, and now he's quite insane.
But you need to wash your hair – so try a little salt.
Those who wash their hair this way might just end up bald,
but find a single salter who's completely lost all sense:
no! you cannot do it, not even one who's dense.

HISTORY

The Mayan Calendar

(Composed on 18 December 2012.   May be sung to the tune of "Rawhide".)

Mayan Mayan Mayan
flyin' flyin' flyin'
from another planet to earth.
They must have had their reasons
to want to see our seasons,
they had a sense of humor and mirth.
Mayan Mayan Mayan
they were always cryin'
missin' the home they left behind.

Gonna end, count the days,
count the days, gonna end
gonna end, count the days
Ma-yan!
Calen-dar, what's it mean?
Why does it have an end?
When it ends, will we too?
Ride 'em in, Ma-yan!

Mayan Mayan Mayan
tryin' tryin' tryin'
wantin' to create so fast
a calendar for trackin'
the days that we are lackin'
for as long as earth would last.
Then they starting packin'
made a fast back-trackin'
departed from their Yucatan home.

They were here, where'd they go?
Where'd they go, they were here.
They were here, where'd they go?
Ma-yan!
Did they know? Did they tell?
Did they tell? Did they know?
Did they know? Did they tell?
Ride 'em in, Mayan!

Mad Anthony Wayne

(Mad Anthony Wayne was an officer in the American Revolutionary Army. Born in 1745, he also served in the House of Representatives from 1791 to 1792. He died in 1796. There have been two theories in wide circulation to explain how he came to be called "mad"; here I present my versions of these two theories, adding also a third theory. Composed between 7 and 18 January 2015, to a waltz rhythm.)

Mad Anthony Wayne, Mad Anthony Wayne,
can it be true that the man was insane?
Mad Anthony Wayne, Mad Anthony Wayne,
how did he come by his name?

Mad Anthony Wayne had a horse called Tremaine,
he and Tremaine used to ride up the lane,
on the left was a garden and right was a plain,
but how did he come by his name?

A story I've heard while riding a train
is that Anthony Wayne had a big bamboo cane –
when regular soldiers disrespected his game,
he'd whip out his cane and inflicted some pain.

According to some, who intone this refrain,
Bee caused the baneful result to his brain,
all she would do is complain and complain,
with time her complaining would drive him insane.

Still others declare that his speech was profane,
bringing him neither advantage nor gain,
but producing sensations of drivel and drain,
of others' repose – oh yes, so insane!

Explanations abound, just like old weather vanes,
explaining what happened to Anthony Wayne.
Here I've recounted just three of the main
versions of how the man went insane.

The Battle of Marston Moor

(Composed on 21 February 2014.)

A battle was fought at Marston Moor in 1644,
the parliament sent its army out to wade in blood and gore.
They managed with mortars, cannon yes, and wielded halberds too,
and short spontoons (not short spittoons) and charged into the dew.
His elegance Prince Rupert led the Royalist forces,
who had the great advantage of wearing silken corsets.
Their weapons and arms could inflict harm, they fought with grace and charm,
Each soldier carried a polished linstock 'cross a leathered arm.
A friar who heard the battle decided he would pray,
and simply walked sans hindrance into the very fray.
He knelt upon a sloping mound and raised his eyes to God,
while all around the wounded fell upon the sod.
He prayed that they would stop their fighting, prayed for all their souls,
but the battle just continued, taking a frightful toll.
Soldiers stabbed each other's bodies, fired off their mortars,
running wildly everywhere, looking for safe quarters.
The battle was fought from early dawn and through the foll'wing night,
when morning came, the air was still, the sun was burning bright.
And all around lay bodies of soldiers of both forces,
and not just of the men involved but also of their horses.
The only person on the field who'd escaped the death and slaying
was the pious friar who continued with his praying.
He walked around to see if any were still living,
But the clash of arms had shown again that it was unforgiving.
The friar then returned to town and rang the chapel bells,
he knew that on the previous day he'd witnessed some of hell.

Joanna the Nutty

(Composed on 13 July 2014.)

Joanna the Nutty was Queen of Castile,
nothing so pleased her as a venison meal,
except for her husband, Philip the Fair,
unless he was riding around on his mare.
She liked when he sat with her, stroking her hair,
but at least 20 ladies liked Philip the Fair.
So to Philip, it seemed only proper and right,
to divide his time equally, daytime and night,
between his betrothed and the ladies he knew,
who patiently waited all lined in a queue.
So handsome was Philip that all through the land,
locals would sing and strike up the band,
whenever he rode to their place of abode,
dismounted and then so boldly he strode.
Joanna and Philip – they knew many things,
such as why snakes and lizards do not have wings.
Joanna denied that the cosmos was boundless,
and considered that theory utterly groundless.
She wanted to demonstrate once and for all,
that the cosmos was bounded by a great granite wall.
Philip thought travel in time was a notion,
sure to provoke a happy commotion.
Some say he succeeded but just for a while,
and brought back some pizzas and served them in style.
Just look at the art and see for yourself,
How Philip kept pizzas lined on his shelf.
Now you have heard all about this royal pair,
'bout Joanna the Nutty and Philip the Fair.
If people should tell you that things were not so,
just tell them that you always know what you know.

Onward, Leif!

(Composed on 9 December 2013. For Torbjørn Knutsen.)

Old Leif Ericson, he was always well met,
attired in leather with a metal helmet.
"Onward, vikings!" he used to like to shout,
"Let's go find a continent, I think I know the route."
So, all his Vikings got aboard a lovely ship,
shouting out "hurray" and a very lively "yip!"
They docked in Greenland, got a little drunk,
worried 'bout the future and sank into a funk.
Then Old Leif Ericson pounded on his chest
and told his merry Vikings "Keep sailing to the West.
If we keep on sailing, we'll surely find that we
end up getting somewhere, wherever that may be."
And so they kept on sailing, fantasizing tuna,
'til their vessel entered into a laguna.
"It's Canada!" Leif bellowed and fell into a trance,
his happy Vikings broke into a dance.
Leif regained his consciousness – that was very brisk –
and told his crew that they should dine on ice-cold lutefisk.
They ate the fish and looked around and got back on their ship,
soon the crew was homeward bound, finished with their trip.
Ericson is famous, not so much his crew,
but everything I've told you here is absolutely true.

The last of the Habsburgs

(Composed on 10 March 2014.)

My credentials are clear, I'm the heir to the throne,
I've already purchased a crown.
I'm moving to Vienna and renting an office,
I'll call it my "palace" downtown.
I'll issue decrees – there'll be chocolate for all,
provided I'm chosen as Kaiser.
The bureaucracy's big, it needs some adjustment:
you can reckon I'll be a downsizer.
One thing's for sure, we don't need to be big –
so what if our empire is small?!
My ambition is large, I want to be loved
by my fellow Austrians all.

The 'real' False Dimitry

(Composed on 30 April 2013; final editing on 10 April 2015.)

Imagine you run into seven Dimitrys,
all of them say they are tsar.
You ask which is really entitled to rule,
their answers don't get you too far.
You ask which are fakers and hope for some insight,
but none will admit to be false.
Your head is soon spinning, you cannot decide –
the seven are dancing a waltz.
But then you determine to ask the whole group
which is the *real* False Dimitry –
you hope that the answers which help you conclude,
without recourse to use of a petri.
The Dimitry's seem baffled, and start to perspire:
you say you are curious – that's all!
But they understand that six of the seven
are false False Dimitrys – so small.

Bowling Tudor style (draft)

(Composed on 21 April 2015, As we learned from Time Team, an archeological program hosted by Tony Robinson, the Tudors were very fond of bowling, and Henry VIII in particular built bowling alleys across Britain. His bowling alley at Hampton Court was 60 meters long, about three times as long as conventional bowling alleys today. May be sung to the tune of "Let's go slumming", a song written by Irving Berlin for the 1937 film "On the avenue".)

Let's go bowling, let's go bowling,
let's go bowling once more Tudor style.
They did it, they do it –
why can't we do it too?
Let's go bowling, go bowling,
bowling Tudor style.

They've got skittles, they've got skittles,
dressed up like a group of dandy French.
If you roll it, just roll it,
maybe you'll get a strike.
Let's go bowling, go bowling,
bowling Tudor style.

CHILDREN'S RHYMES

On Dumpledy-Down

(Composed between 20 September and 10 October 2013; for Priscilla Ringrose.)

On Dumpledy-Down near the church in the vale,
chipmunks and squirrels with big bushy tales,
gather and blather of all sorts of things,
like Shepherdly-Shemp and the songs that he sings.

This Saturday morn', from out of the woods,
come foxes all donning their red riding hoods.
They're looking so proper, just waving their fans,
but where are they going and what are their plans?

It's Shepherdly-Shemp that they're wanting to see:
on that all the foxes entirely agree.
They're eager to hear him trilling his notes,
and want his advice on subjects remote.

On Landerly-Lane they hear serenading:
it's Shepherdly-Shemp and his tune is cascading,
downward and upward, it's easy to hear
why it's his singing brings everyone cheer.

But curious foxes need also advice:
would it be useful and would it be nice
if they would offer a counseling service?
Shemp thinks that's great, no one should be nervous.

So, on Dumpledy-Down they're setting up shop,
giving advice to all who will stop.
What should I wear? What should I do?
Just ask the foxes: they'll give you a clue.

Alice in Limerickland

(Composed 24—27 December 2013; inspired by Lewis Carroll's "Alice in Wonderland" or, more precisely, by seeing three minutes of a ballet on the theme of Carroll's "Alice in Wonderland" on Norwegian television on 24 December.)

There once was a maiden named Alice,
who lived in a great crystal palace.
She fell down a hole
that was made by a mole,
or maybe a rabbit, so callous.

A rabbit so white made of plastic
had limbs that were strong and elastic,
while she followed its tail,
it ran up the trail,
into a great hall dynastic.

A green caterpillar was there,
and advised Alice she should beware
of mushrooms around
that grew on the ground:
if she ate them she'd have quite a scare.

Then she encountered a fungus,
she ate it and grew quite humungus.
But that was not all,
since she also shrank small.
The fungus was called omphalotus.

A tea party with a mad hatter
was occasion for laughter and chatter –
"Would you like some more tea?"
"Why that cannot be,
because I've had none, for that matter."

The March Hare just stood for a while,
then replied with a curious smile,
"More than nothing is more,
so don't be a bore,
just accept some more tea without bile."

'Twas tea that she drank from a cup,
was invited to join them for sup
by the hatter and hare,
a jolly gay pair,
just living alone with their pup.

The garden whose roses were painted
had paint fumes and Alice near fainted.
All roses are red,
all violets are blue.
These painters were sorely demainted.

"Why do you paint the flow'rs red,
when a rose can be yellow instead?"
The painters replied
that they merely complied
with commands at the price of their heads.

"Well, none of this makes any sense,
no matter your fine recompense,"
thought Alice aloud,
but the painters were cowed
and continued their work looking tense.

With that Alice let out a laugh
and wandered on down a steep path,
'til she got to a bay
where a game was in play,
with Her Highness, the old psychopath.

The Queen was already at play
at a vigorous game of croquet,

but the rules of the game
were never the same,
when the Queen was the host of the day.

For a mallet she used a flamingo
and grabbed the poor bird by its dingo,
then swung at the ball,
shouting "Death to you all!"
but what did that mean in her lingo?

Alice, of course, had to query,
"How is it Your Highness is merry,
while condemning to death
in a frivolous breath
all present, who find you quite scary?"

But Highness was clearly insane,
especially, you see, in her brain,
ignored what was asked,
and instead she basked
in her glory and spoke this refrain:

"When sheep are fluorescent they glow
on the mountain tops up by the snow;
thanks to jelly fish genes
they glow pink and green –
just ask me how I can know?"

But Alice thought this was absurd,
did not believe even one word,
since the Queen was insane
right in her brain,
and soon forgot what she had heard.

Just then a large cat appeared,
and all round the sans culottes cheered,
since this Cheshire cat knew
everything through and through,
and had beautiful whiskers and beard.

"The truth is much truer than fiction,"
said the cat with most elegant diction.
"So say what you mean,
come on and come clean,
and say it with honest conviction."

"OK," said Alice undaunted
and explained to the cat that she wanted
to just understand
the rules of this land
and not to be mocked or be taunted.

"Well, censorship – that's what that is,"
said the cat and, continuing, "Ms.,
you don't have the right
to not be polite.
And besides, just what is your biz?"

But Alice had no time to answer
for just then a talented dancer
sprang onto the floor,
then leaped out the door,
but let in a calm necromancer.

This "necro" would talk to the dead
whom clearly he heard in his head.
But others could not
even make out the plot,
since they heard only what "necro" said.

A crocodile back from the dead,
was whispering something, he said,
about flowers that talked
and fishes that walked
on their fins when they got out of bed.

"No, this is impossibly crazy,"
said Alice, her mind growing hazy,

"It's time to wake up,
and yes to take up
my chores and to stop being lazy."

And with that our Alice awoke
in a room that was filled with pink smoke:
that seemed a bit strange
but life's about change,
and at least she was back in her poke.

Knightsalot of the Round Table

(Composed on 17 September 2013.)

Sir Lancelot, he had a lance,
Sir Notalot did not.
Sir Laughalot, he did just that,
Sir Eatalot was fat.
And Kingalot was Arthur,
who planned a lot and more:
'twas he who would determine
what the future held in store.

Bedouin

(Composed on 30 April 2016. The last two lines were added on 1 May, with final editing on 21 May 2016.)

Bedouin Bedouin Bedouin priest –
he's prepared a Bedouin feast
Bedouin Bedouin Bedouin nun –
she's so holy, she's number one.
Bedouin Bedouin Bedouin Bedouin
Bedouin (clap clap) Bedouin (clap)

Bedouin Bedouin Bedouin aisle –
every Bedouin makes me smile
Bedouin Bedouin Bedouin saint –
I'm so happy I could faint.
Bedouin Bedouin Bedouin Bedouin
Bedouin (clap clap) Bedouin (clap)
Bedouin Bedouin Bedouin Bedouin
Bedouin Bedouin (clap clap clap).

Danger! Beware of the coconuts!

(Composed on 1 March 2015, immediately after dinner with Sophus, Olav, Eskild, and Ewa. Dedicated to Ewa and Eskild, who inspired this verse, with their tales of Thailand.)

Coconuts, coconuts in the sky
coconuts, coconuts, way up high
please don't fall down on my head
that would likely knock me dead.
I don't have coconuts in my garage
but I saw them there once, it was just a mirage.
I don't have coconuts in my yard,
but if I did, I'd be on guard
'cause coconuts fall quite without warning
especially daytime, nighttime or morning,
so wear a helmet every day
and scare the coconuts away!

ANIMALS

Some of my best friends…

(Composed on 15 May 2014 at St. Olav's Hospital, while waiting for a routine check-up.)

Some of my best friends are pigeons –
innocent creatures, whose great delight is to be fed.
I'll grant you that, for pigeons,
the whole world is a toilet.
But to go to the park
and sit on a public bench,
feeding the pigeons,
is surely one of the great pleasures in life –
at least on a sunny day.

My neighbor worships my dog

(Composed on 1 May 2014, while waiting for the sun to go down.)

Tim my neighbor's big and burly,
was a cop, retired early,
misses chases with his siren,
bought a toy and did some wirin'.
Bought himself an ice-cream van,
then proceeded with his plan:
turns his makeshift siren on,
has his water pistol drawn,
flashing lights both green and yellow,
and on his megaphone he bellows:
"THIS IS NOT THE POLICE.
DO NOT PULL OVER TO THE SIDE OF THE ROAD.
REPEAT: THIS IS NOT THE POLICE.
DO NOT PULL OVER TO THE SIDE OF THE ROAD."

Tim has a dog but prefers mine,
he thinks that my pooch is divine.
Every night I hear him praying
and with his hymns he is conveying
joyous signs of adulation
for our doggie (a Dalmatian).
What he wants is reinstatement
in the force – there's no abatement
in his litany for help,
but my doggie, who's no whelp,
ignores his prayers and his pleas –
he's busy brushing off some fleas.
I'm worried 'bout my neighbor, Tim,
but I'm not sure what to do for him:
meanwhile Tim continues odd,
worshipping my pooch as God.

Caring for your jellyfish

(Composed on 17 April 2014. For Jennifer Bailey.)

Congratulations on purchasing your new jellyfish!
It will bring you years of pleasure, but
there are a few things you should know:
first, jellyfish are gregarious.
If you want a happy jellyfish, you should
make sure that your jellyfish has lots of company,
about 20 would be right.
Since they congregate in schools,
they are happy in swimming pools.
Second, as you surely see,
they're used to swimming in the sea.
Fill your pool with ocean water,
sea weed, anemones, and then your jellyfish.
Fish, crustaceans, and some plankton
are the things they like to eat.
Every week add 50 pounds
of fishes, plankton and some meat.
Third, there is just one more thing,
jellyfish are happy when you sing.
They like harps and violins and organs too,
do this for your jellyfish and they will be forever true.

My little 'font' goldfish

(Composed on 2 April 2015; final editing on 10 April 2015.)

I have a fish tank full of fish, surrounded by a frame,
and one thing that I know for sure is each fish has a name.
Monotype Corsiva is a most curvaceous fish, while little cute
Verdana makes me think of Lillian Gish.
Another fish that swims around is known as Times New Roman –
I think I saw him trying once to build a little snow man.
TNR is best of friends with my fish Tahoma,
I took them on an outing once to see downtown Tacoma:
they weren't impressed and said no thanks
and stayed inside their tank.
They didn't care for traffic lights
and took no note of city sights.
Palatino Linotype is tall and proud and almost never late,
and hangs around a happy sea horse, known as Cooperplate.
My memory is sharp, not dim,
I know that most fish like to swim,
except for Cambria, that piscine maid,
who likes to slumber in the shade.
Then there's bright Calibri – a fish without serifs –
accompanied by Baskerville, always wearing briefs.
But of all my many fish, most striking is Old English Text,
whose soothing minstrel singing always calms me when I'm vexed.

POLITICS AND MEDIA

Don't you be sexing, here in Uganda

(Inspired by Uganda's draconian law, mandating life imprisonment for gays and lesbians. Composed on 1 March 2014.)

Stick to the straight, don't you go wanda,
or we'll stick you in prison here in Uganda.
Sex, we've determined, means babies galore
and we have enough, we're not needing more.
So, for now, homosexuals – we lock them all up,
but later the straights – their time will be up.
Don't you be sexing, here in Uganda,
sex is bad business, you don't have to wanda.
Castration's a sacrament, give you our blessing,
once you have had it, there'll be no more messing.
Say "hysterectomy" – that's a solution:
this is salvation and not persecution.
We're giving the country back to the beasts,
we think they're OK, we like people the least.

Radio Walla Walla, best news team in the business, or: In a democracy, we need informed citizens

(Composed on 21 March 2014; augmented on 28 March 2014.)

Down in downtown Walla Walla
we're the best team bringing news,
whether it's about the traffic
or the latest trend in blues
or Farmer Bill's potato crop,
we're bringing info you can use.
Train wrecks, wars, and car collisions,
also when a bridge collapses,
earthquakes in some distant land,
politicians' crazy lapses,
sports results and latest movies,
advertisements for new sandals,
freakish fractures down in France,
what's the latest in sex scandals,
all the new incarcerations,
who's released and on probation,
murders, arson, forest fires,
crime waves and electric storms,
these are things that really matter:
just tune in and be informed.

Chick chicky boom

(Composed on 23 September 2014. This is set to the tune of "Cuban Pete", a Cuban rumba song composed by Joseph Norman in 1936, popularized by Desi Arnaz, who sang the song in the 1946 film "Cuban Pete", and more recently sung by Jim Carrey in the 1994 action comedy film "The Mask".)

This is the evening news,
we have knowledge that you can use.
When we play a commercial we go,
chick chicky boom, chick chicky boom.

There's been a forest fire,
so yes we're gonna inquire,
what people think when they lose their houses,
chick chicky boom.

Their houses are up in flames,
our journalist asks, how do they feel,
when they have lost everything that they owned.
He does not know,
because his brain is ever so slow,
and he never thinks,
he cannot see what's obvious to all.

So if you like to hear
some knowledge that you can use,
we can teach you on evening news,
chick chicky boom, chick chicky boom.

Baa-baa, mad king

(Inspired by recalling the old nursery rhyme, "Baa-baa, black sheep", the earliest surviving version of which goes back to 1731. Composed on 10-11 October 2014).

"Baa-baa, mad king, have you any rules?"
"Lots of them and a ton of fools,
who do whatever I tell them to.
You wouldn't believe what I've put them through!"
"Baa-baa, mad king, have you any rules?"
"Lots of them and a ton of fools."

"Baa-baa, mad king, have you any canes?"
"Yes, I need them to bash in the brains
of little men who think they know what's what –
since they don't, they're quickly caught!"
"Baa-baa, mad king, have you any canes?"
"Yes, I need them to bash in your brains."

"Baa-baa, mad king, tell me what's the sort
of noble men who sit in your court."
"Sychophants I like the best, they deserve the royal crest.
But obedience quite suffices, the opposite are some nasty vices."
"Baa-baa, mad king, what's your fav'rite sport?"
"Keeping bishops silent in my court."

"Baa-baa, mad king, we are all your sheep:
give us orders or we shall weep.
All we want is to obey,
we are ready now, today.
Baa-baa, mad king, we are all your sheep:
give us orders or we shall weep."

In praise of Erna

(Composed on 12 October 2014.)

We put our countrywoman – or countryman, if you prefer – Erna
in charge of our budget and asked her to rule wisely.
She promised to increase the funding for kindergartens,
but that was just a liesly.
She cut the taxes – hip hooray!
to make that work, she slashed the funding
for libraries, newspapers, music and the arts –
now that was cunning.
We saw that coming, but we thought we didn't care,
but now we do. But what of the money saved?
A tupence for every ordinary citizen, a million for every rich bloke –
if you object, then you're depraved.
Hurrah for Erna! She has a vision: she is Reagan reincarnate:
so, lower taxes for the rich.
Is that perverse? Or is it a plan to take our country
into the ditch?

Choir wars with flutes

(Composed on 28 March 2014, while still radioactive.)

When two nations think of war, to resolve some fresh disputes,
why not set aside their arms and solve the problem with some flutes?
Bring out choirs, drums, and fifes – the better music wins the day,
some impartial judge be found: he will have the final say.
If you think of conflicts past, surely you will soon agree
that always those who fought for right had the better pedigree
for music and performance too, and that their concerts were the best.
World War One and World War Two, who can doubt they'd pass the test?

Silvio Berlusconi's paradise

(Composed on 30 December 2013, in the car, while Chris drove us home from Frosta.)

Welcome, cittadini, to my party –
take a glass and let's get starty!
Fill it up and take a swig,
are you feeling carefree and big?
Hey bunga-bunga, yes bunga-bunga.
You have landed in bunga-bunga land.

Find a sofa, just relax,
get some resting on your backs.
What d'you want now – girls or boys?
One of each? Just not too much noise!
Oi bunga-bunga, si bunga-bunga!
You have landed in bunga-bunga land!

I'm prime minister, I've got immunity,
I do what I like and with impunity:
Ladies in my car and I'm driving fast,
these good times are going to last.
Oi bunga-bunga, si bunga-bunga,
I'm the King of Bunga-Bunga Land.

A guide on how to riot

(Composed on 28 June 2014.)

So you want to riot – well, here's a little guide:
if you want to riot, it's got to be outside.
If you stay inside your bedroom – here's a little clue –
it doesn't count as rioting, no matter what you do.
You can throw around the pillows and overturn the bed,
even shoot a round of bullets through a loaf of bread.
You can blame your little teddy bear for your current woe,
but none of this is rioting – believe me, as I know.

You've got to do some shouting, slogans and the like,
and always do some running: you're not just on a hike.
Banners are essential, hoist them to the sky,
and drink some alcohol before, to help you think you're high.
But most important – this I know – it likely would be best
to wear a metal helmet and a bullet-proof vest.
Now you're ready, grab your banner, go out on the street,
shout and curse and run a bit, on your dancing feet.

SUPERHEROES

The Adventures of Retread Rabbit

(Composed on 14-15 January 2014. This verse is built on the template of the introduction to "Adventures of Superman", a television series which starred George Reeves as Superman, and ran from 1951 to 1958.)

Faster than a speeding cockroach,
more powerful than a ripe carrot,
able to leap over bales of hay in a single bound:
Look, up in the lettuce patch --
it's a bird, it's a plane, it's Retread Rabbit!

Yes, it's Retread Rabbit,
strange visitor from another lettuce patch,
who came to this lettuce patch
with powers and abilities far beyond those of other rabbits.

Retread Rabbit,
who can change the way we think about rivers,
bend carrots in his bare paws, and who,
disguised as Rehab Rabbit, mild-mannered reporter
for a Great Metropolitan Newspaper for Rabbits,
fights a never-ending battle
for the environment, sustainability, and the preservation of species.

Rabbit Hood

(Composed on 17 January 2014. Constructed on the template of the introduction to "The Adventures of Robin Hood", a British television series, starring Richard Greene, which aired from 1955 to 1960.)

He called his clan of rabbits
to a nearby rabbit patch,
they vowed to keep their lettuce clean and fresh.
They chased away the insects
that were threatening their stash,
and still found plenty of time to sing:
"Rabbit Hood, Rabbit Hood, carrot in his hand.
Rabbit Hood, Rabbit Hood – no food that is canned.
Feared by the bugs, loved by the hares,
Rabbit Hood, Rabbit Hood, Rabbit Hood."

The Lone Rabbit

(Composed on 18 January 2014. This verse is built, in part, on the template of the introduction to "The Lone Ranger", a television series which starred Clayton Moore as the Lone Ranger, and ran from 1949 to 1957.)

The Lone Rabbit to the rescue!
A fiery rabbit with the speed of light, a cloud of dust,
and a hearty "Hi ho, carrots!"
The Lone Rabbit rides again!
With his trusty side-kick, Wadley the Weasel,
this artistic rabbit sets down his easel,
whenever a damsel or fellow's in distress,
whenever there's need to clean up some mess,
rounding up looters and rotten polluters:
The Lone Rabbit rides again!

Mighty Rabbit's on the way!

(This verse, composed on 19 October 2016, is built on the template of the theme song to "Mighty Mouse", a television series which aired from 1955 through 1967. Mighty Mouse was a character created by Paul Terry of Terrytoons Studio for 20th Century Fox and first appeared in 1942 under the nom de guerre "Super Mouse". In the years 1942-1961, Mighty Mouse appeared in 80 films. Among his many powers, Mighty Mouse was able to turn back time. The theme song to the "Mighty Mouse" television series was written by Philip Scheib and Marshall Barer around 1955.)

Rats and termites never hang around,
when Mighty Rabbit's on the ground.
"Here I come to save the day!"
sings Mighty Rabbit on his way.
Yes ma'am, when bad guys try to fool
the public, then it's time for school:
citizens must be informed
so that their thinking is not deformed.
Mighty Rabbit will teach the folk who don't have a clue,
because he has the answers and he's ready to do
whatever it takes to get us through.
We're keeping lettuce right on hand
and are ready for his song,
"Here I come to save the day!"
That means that Mighty Rabbit's on the way.
When candidates without experience,
claim to have a better insight,
Mighty Rabbit's on the way,
and he won't give up the fight!

Radioactive me

(Composed on 26 March 2014, in anticipation of a PET-CT scan at the Royal Hospital in Oslo.)

Radioactive in my veins,
soon it will infect my brains.
I'll be reading people's minds,
see through walls and opaque blinds.
I will soar above the clouds
at supersonic speed – that's loud!
I'll be lifting tons of metal,
Whistling louder than your kettle.
I'll be writing books at speeds
faster than a person reads.
Superhuman, well, why not?
Radioactive is my lot.

RAMBLINGS

About Petter Jenssen

(Written at high speed just before noon on 8 January 2015.)

Where is Petter Jensen and who is he anyway?
His name comes up from time to time,
but we have no information.
What is his line of work?
Where does his live?
Is he honest?
What are his politics?
Where is Petter Jensen and who is he anyway?
We have no information.

I think I saw him the other day –
only problem: I don't know what he looks like,
my partner has mentioned him a few times,
or maybe I simply misheard –
because she knows nothing about the man
and has never met him.
We are not even sure he exists,
but if he does not exist,
why do we know his name?
Where is Petter Jensen and who is he anyway?
We have no information.

Maybe he is a politician, hiding his views,
but he won't get our vote
if we know nothing about him
and we don't even see his name on the ballot.
Maybe we should call telephone information
and ask if there is someone called Petter Jensen
in our country.
Where is Petter Jensen and who is he anyway?
We have no information.

Yo-ho yo, a professor's life for me

(Hammered together during January-February 2016. With thanks to song writers for the ride at "Disneyland" in Anaheim, where the song "Yo-ho, yo-ho, a pirate's life for me" was first performed for the public. The entire ride, complete with singing, is posted at https://www.youtube.com/watch?v=Uv7APUxrebw.)

Yo-ho yo, a professor's life for me,
we teach, we read, we write, we think, we're working through the night
and other people read our work
and then they tell us we're right!

Yo-ho yo, a professor's life for me
our students always come to class, they read assignments twice
and when they sit for their exams
their answers more than suffice!

Yo-ho yo, a professor's life for me
I read a book the other day that's full of lively thoughts,
I think I'll let those thoughts sink in
while sailing around on my yacht.

Yo-ho, yo-ho, yo-ho ho!

I just can't help myself

(Composed on 19 November 2013; inspired by "Dreamhouse", a splendifarious televisual experience.)

Thick rubber membrane, sitting on the roof,
cuddly little doggies going "woof woof!"
I'm sitting on my rocker, staring at the clouds,
Watching people I didn't like lying under shrouds.
I just can't help myself, I think I need some okra,
While I sit and wait, I drink a little mocca.
78 rpm's are spinning round and round,
While I'm here I'm resting somewhere near the ground.
Thick rubber membrane, sitting on the roof,
cuddly little doggies going "woof woof!"
Sometimes I imagine I'm living on the moon,
as far as I'm aware, there's still a lot of room.
Rents are low, crime is low, but dating is a problem,
Not so many girls and boys, not even just a goblin.
I just can't help myself, I've got to give a speech,
there are a ton of lessons I'm ready now to teach.
People need instruction, and I am qualified,
to tell them what they're doing wrong, and how their brains are fried.
Thick rubber membrane, sitting on the roof,
cuddly little doggies going "woof woof!"

anARchisTs 4 gOOd grammar

(Composed on 12 October 2014.)

psychedelic anARchisTs
sparkling at night, grazing by day
phrasing their way to
grammatical paradISe –
anarchism, YES!
but not in grammar:
there must be rules,
the anarchist grammar enforcer
says,
he knows,
his grammar is sparkling
also by day –
yours can be too

Just so

(Composed on 16 September 2013.)

When she sits, she sits just so –
I tell you this, so that you know.
When she reads, she reads just so –
she's not too fast and not too slow.
When she works – what? need you ask?
She works just so on every task.
And when she goes to bed at night,
she sleeps just so with covers tight.

For persons struggling with French words

(Composed on 14 November 2013, at 5:25 a.m.)

So you like to watch ballette,
leave your car with the valette,
then you drive to your chalette
in your shiny chevrolette:
there you dine on foods gourmette,
learning French along the wet.

You are not an individual

(Composed on 14 May 2014, on a KLM flight from Amsterdam to Trondheim. This verse is not a reflection on the excellent service I received from KLM staff.)

Remember this: you are not an individual,
your personality is purely residual.
You have no opinions, you always agree,
you always like whatever you see.
You always believe whatever you're told,
you don't have a clue what it means to be bold.
You're always ready to smile and to nod,
you simply ignore anybody who's odd.

And

(Composed in June 2014.)

There once was a limerick and
it was stylish and elegant and,
with a rhyme in each line
and a meter so fine,
and.

Jack and Jim went up the hill – no, that's not right

(Composed on 18 July 2014.)

Jack and Jim went to the rim of Bourbon Hill with Daniel,
they took a swig and did a jig, and saw a cocker spaniel.
Johnny walked around the beam, while Glenn Moe Rangie halted,
but all of them agreed on this: that whiskey should be malted.

Stealing Being and Time

(Composed on 5 February 2015, in the evening.)

The police have caught the scalawag
who perpetrated many a crime,
he'd been breaking into professors' offices
and stealing their copies of *Being and Time*.
Heidegger's not to everyone's taste,
few can grasp his "being there".
But this scalawag had stashed
520 copies in his lair.
Some were highlighted in yellow,
others underlined in red,
some were still so crisp and clean,
'twas clear that they had ne'er been read.
And now this criminal's been brought to court,
insanity will be his plea.
I guess that I'd agree with that,
if it were up to me.

Procrastinator

(Composed in the middle of the night, 29/30 March 2015.)

Tomorrow I will think a great thought – today I'm a little busy.
Tomorrow I will be a little busy – today I'm resting.
Tomorrow I will rest – today I'm thinking a great thought.

The Great Stink of 1858

(Inspired by a short report on the Discovery Channel & composed on 6-7 April 2015 to the tune to "Somewhere over the rainbow". This song, immortalized by Judy Garland in the 1939 film, "The Wizard of Oz", was the result of a collaboration between Harold Arlen, who wrote the music, and E. Y. Harburg, who wrote the original lyrics.)

Sewage into the river – water's brown,
rubbish into the Thames, now that was in London town.
Debris into the river – just don't drink,
and the refuse you discard produces an awful stink.

One day the city cleaned it up
and dredged the river end to end for safety.
That was in 1858 –
who knew the troubles would abate?
And now we filtrate…

Somewhere over the sewage, blue birds fly,
they ignore all the stench, oh,
why then, oh why can't I?

Sewage into the river – water's brown,
please don't swim in the river, please it would make you frown.
Flush your waste in the river, it won't sink,
and whatever you do there, make sure that you don't drink.

Bonk Bonk Bonk

(Except for a few phrases, this is complete nonsense, and has no intended meaning. If you think that there is some hidden meaning here, you are deluding yourself. Composed on 6 April 2015, during a brief intermission in my afternoon nap.)

Ausgetrüpft mit krünnen Bopfen,
in den krieben, vieben Sopfen
und wir behen tünde Vopfen –
ja, das ist ein Bonk Bonk Bonk.

In den Torgen aufgeborgen
möhen wir und nicht gesorgen,
und am Ende tachtgeworgen,
immer wieder Bonk Bonk Bonk.

Ja, Sie kwehen, ja zu brehen
jeder sill ein Tisschen lehen
und am Schluss boch sieder jähen,
blanzen um den Bonk Bonk Bonk.

Petrol station greeter

(Composed on 17 April 2015, upon waking up. Inspired by memories of actual petrol station greeters in Sapporo, Japan, where we spent the academic year 1993-94; in Sapporo, typically, a petrol station would have at least four persons on hand to greet drivers as they pulled into the station, and to assist them in reentering traffic after the extensive service was complete.)

Philip and Philippa
traveled down to Kreta,
Philip told Philippa
that he was a greeter.
"What on earth's a greeter?"
asked him now Philippa.
"When you're getting petrol,
you're going to need a greeter
to bring you in the station,"
Philip told Philippa.
"And if you start to weepa,
and need some consolation,
help is from the greeter
at the petrol station.
He's stronger than a sweeper,
his thoughts are always deeper –
I'm proud to be a greeter
at the petrol station."